THE
Archive Photographs
SERIES
AROUND
EXETER

No. 226 High Street, Exeter, c.1955. Formerly the home of the *Express & Echo* and the *Western Gazette*, it was puchased by J.Lyons & Co. Ltd when the newspapers moved to Sidwell Street. It was once the home of Simon Snow, city merchant and Mayor (1653), who represented Exeter in the Long Parliament which commenced in 1640. The building is thought to date from 1567 and has a lengthy connection with the newspaper world. It passed through several hands until bought by Robert Trewman (a good name for a newspaper owner), one of the original proprietors of the *Exeter Flying Post* which was published there until 1886. It then housed the *Devon Weekly Times*, the *Western Echo* and the *Devon Evening Echo*, the last two amalgamating, and finally the *Express & Echo*, the first copy of which was published from the building on 1 October 1904.

THE
Archive Photographs
SERIES
AROUND
EXETER

Compiled by
Les Berry and Gerald Gosling

CHALFORD

First published 1996
Copyright © Les Berry and Gerald Gosling, 1996

The Chalford Publishing Company
St Mary's Mill, Chalford,
Stroud, Gloucestershire, GL6 8NX

ISBN 0 7524 0323 0

Typesetting and origination by
The Chalford Publishing Company
Printed in Great Britain by
Redwood Books, Trowbridge

Contents

High Street, Exeter, in the 1930s, with St Stephen's church on the extreme right. Bobby's, a leading name in Exeter's commercial world and a drapers of some repute, suffered along with the rest of upper High Street during the 1941 bombings. It rose, after a spell in Fore Street, phoenix-like, albeit nowhere near as handsomely, on the corner of Sidwell Street and New North Road, and is now Debenham's departmental store. Deller's main restaurant in Cathedral Close (see p. 25) later moved to Bedford Circus and advertised itself as being 'one minute from the Trams'. For the shopper too weary to make that walk, their cafe and tea rooms in the middle background were very popular in later years but, sadly, are now only a fond memory for an annually decreasing number of older Exonians.

Introduction

Ever since the Romans reached the banks of the River Exe and liked what they saw of the bluff looking out across the water towards Dartmoor, Exeter has been a city of some importance. The Romans called it *Isca Damnorium* and to them it was the edge of the world, their 'Wild West'. They did go beyond but had little enthusiasm for Dartmoor and the remote, gaunt Cornish wastes, and they made little effort to educate the few Britons who lived out there about the benefits of living under the *Pax Romana*. From that time on, Exeter has stood at the gateway of English history. Saxons and Danes followed Rome and then the Conqueror himself was forced to come west to subdue the city which was already laying claim to its later motto *Semper Fidelis* (Ever Faithful). It stayed faithful. Henry's daughter, the Empress Matilda, found it so, and it took the usurping Stephen three months to break down its resistance. The Yorkist would-be usurper Perkin Warbeck attacked the city in 1497, Henry VII arriving later in person to say thank you. The Prayer Book Rebellion, Roundhead and Cavalier, Monmouth, and William of Orange all left their mark on the city. As indeed did the Luftwaffe, which in World War Two destroyed the city's architectural heart – but not its real heart. The capital of a county which produced Drake, Raleigh, Hawkins, Grenville, Jackie Churchill, the great Duke of Marlborough, Ronald Falcon Scott and thousands like them could never lose that.

Happily, the Luftwaffe, although it used it as the aiming point for its bombs, failed to do any serious damage to Exeter's 'Jewel in its Crown' – the magnificent cathedral of St Peter and its unique and distinctive transeptal towers (if you discount the faithful copy at nearby Ottery St Mary). All great jewels are improved by great settings; St Peter's is no exception. A few yards away is the bustle and noise of a crowded city; in the Close all is quiet and dignified, the cathedral not dominating its neighbours but blending in with them in a way no modern architect could even begin to understand. There are many treasures there, none greater than the massive west front and window.

There is, of course, more to Exeter than just St Mary's. Much was lost for ever in the bombing – Sidwell Street, Upper High Street, Bedford Circus, especially Bedford Circus. And, sadly, most was replaced with hideous examples of architectural vandalism on a scale that must have made many an old builder turn, no writhe, in his grave. But much remains: old streets, old houses, the superb Guildhall, some splendid churches and, even if it is outside the scope of this book, the red, red earth of Devon with its gentle countryside all around.

Les Berry and Gerald Gosling have shown us much of a city's past in this book, especially the views of streets denied the modern generation by the Luftwaffe. They are to be commended for their efforts.

Frank Huddy
Chard, 1996

One
High Street
and Sidwell Street

Exeter's High Street at the turn of the century. Of special interest here are the shop awnings, which were fixed to poles on the edge of the pavement, and the state of the street, which appears to have a swept crossing place (the nearest cart is just crossing it).

High Street, c.1908.

High Street, c.1935, with St Petrock's church in the background. The six-bell peel in the church was said to be the lightest in England. The two shops immediately to the right of the church are now Reject Jeans and Bradford & Bingley. The Fifty Shilling Tailors and the Ocean offices were demolished to make way for road widening at the junction of High Street and South Street (see p. 49).

High Street, c.1909. Timothy White's stood to the left of the entrance to Gandy Street. It was, happily, an area which escaped the damage suffered by other parts of the city centre during wartime bombing.

The Head Post Office (right) in High Street, c.1909. Destroyed during the war, the city's main post office later moved to Bedford Street (see p. 29).

St Lawrence's church, High Street, Exeter, c.1920. Just visible on the right is the '6' of the Devon & Somerset Stores' 246 High Street number. The British Shoe Company became Ann the Milliners. St Lawrence's, which, along with all this part of High Street, was destroyed during the war, dated from at least the twelfth century. The handsome south porch had been constructed from the materials of a conduit that was erected near the church in 1590 but removed in 1674.

Both Garton & King Ltd and Pinder & Tuckwell are holding closing down sales at their Exeter High Street premises, which dates the picture to the mid-1930s. By the outbreak of World War Two, a certain F.W. Woolworth & Co. Ltd's bazaar had arrived at nos 190 and 191 High Street.

High Street, c.1920. This picture is worth including if for no other reason than to give modern residents some idea of the architectural gems that were destroyed in upper High Street, including, peeping out in the background, St Lawrence's church.

The Theatre Royal, Longbrook Street, Exeter, c.1957.

The audience leaving the Theatre Royal after an Exeter Pleasant Sunday Afternoon Service in around 1909.

Castle Hotel, Castle Street, Exeter, presumably during the 1897 Diamond Jubilee celebrations. It was destroyed in the 1942 blitz.

High Street, c.1949, with St Stephen's church in the background. Colson & Co's and Barratt's shops now form form part of Dingle's stores. The Commer van, which looks more like an armoured car, is a survivor from pre-war days (probably 1935).

Webb & Son of 231 and 232 High Street, Exeter, with branches at Plymouth and Bristol, were manufacturers (they called themselves 'actual' manufacturers in a 1913 advert) of 'High-Class Fancy Leather Goods, Suit Cases, Travelling Trunks, Dressing Cases, etc.' They claimed to be the largest manufacturers and to possess the most complete stocks of leather goods in the provinces, and, in words redolent of the glories of Empire, made 'Trunks for the Colonies'.

The Guildhall, High Street, seen here in around 1908, was erected on the site of a former Guildhall in 1330, the frontage being constructed between 1592 and 1595. Despite subsequent renovations, it has not been altered since. Claims are made for its being the oldest civic building in Britain. The roof, which dates from 1468-9, has 'Bear and Ragged Staff' corbels.

High Street in the early 1960s, after the rebuilding of the higher end of the street.

Exeter's Sidwell Street *en fête* in 1905, when the city said 'Goodbye' to the old horse-drawn trams. This picture was taken by well-known Exeter photographer R. Barrett.

A packed High Street greets the opening of Exeter Electric Tramways on 4 April 1905. A private horse-drawn tramway was operated from Heavitree to St Sidwell's as early as 1882, and this was followed in 1883 by a line from St David's station to the Blackboy. The horse-drawn trams never really caught on, and, after a vote by the ratepayers which was nearly 5-1 in favour, the new system was inaugurated by the Mayor (Councillor Perry).

The first electric trams pass along a crowded High Street.

Sidwell Street, Exeter, c.1910. The White Lion Hotel was a popular drinking spot for many years.

Green & Son, 25-26 High Street, Exeter, were Court Dressmakers, Costumiers, Milliners and Fancy Drapers of some repute, and at the time of this picture, in 1913, had been in Exeter for over eighty years. Not unnaturally, they made much of the fact that their premises stood on the site of the old New Inn, one-time principal inn of the city. The ceiling of the Apollo Room, one of Green & Son's showrooms, was a masterpiece built in 1689 by Thomas Lane, a plasterer, at a rate of five shillings per yard. He was paid £50 in all.

High Street in the 1920s, when the car was becoming a nuisance to the tram. Or was it the other way round? The athletic outfitters, Jn Webber & Sons, later moved to Queen Street. Dellers' have a confectionery branch next door. This does not appear to be a special occasion and the ladies summer dresses certainly rule out Christmas shopping, so a crowded High Street is not a modern phenomenon!

The Church of All Hallows, Exeter, c.1896. This stood on the corner of Goldsmith Lane looking out into the High Street, but was demolished in 1906.

Looking down High Street from the corner of Queen Street. The blacked-out headlights on the right hand bus (this particular type was introduced in 1941) and the 'Savings' poster suggest this was taken during World War Two, even if there are not as many people in uniform as one might expect.

Bedford Circus, c.1945, when the ruins of the 1942 blitz had been cleared and the site was awaiting redevelopment. In the meantime, obvious car parking spaces were available. In the left rear, Catherine Street leads into the Cathedral Close.

Even with the Cathedral as a landmark in the background, it is difficult to place the actual position of this bomb site in around 1942-43. The clues are the boards telling shoppers where the various shops and businesses have gone. Edward Sebley (left) was a gentleman's outfitter at 1b High Street; Troulans, ophthalmic opticians, were at no. 2, as were Levy's, the ladies hairdressers.

The New London Hotel in London Inn Square, Exeter, seen above in around 1914, was demolished in 1936 and the Savoy Cinema (seen below in 1958) took its place. It was in its own turn also demolished.

Cathedral Close, c.1908. The close was formerly the city's burial ground. It was first enclosed by a wall in 1286, when it had seven gates.

The Globe Hotel, Cathedral Yard, c.1919. St Mary Major's church on the right, which dated from the twelfth century, was rebuilt in 1865-68 on a site a little to the west of the original Norman building.

Exeter, Clarence Hotel and Dellers Cafe.

Deller's first cafe in Exeter was in the Cathedral Close, where it is seen, above, in 1904. It later moved to Bedford Circus, where the orchestra played three times daily and the cafe claimed in Edwardian adverts to be 'one minute from Trams'. For those too tired to leave the High Street, there was a confectionery branch at 48-49 High Street (see p. 6) where the tea rooms were a great favourite with the shoppers. The picture below shows part of the interior of the Cathedral Close premises in around 1913.

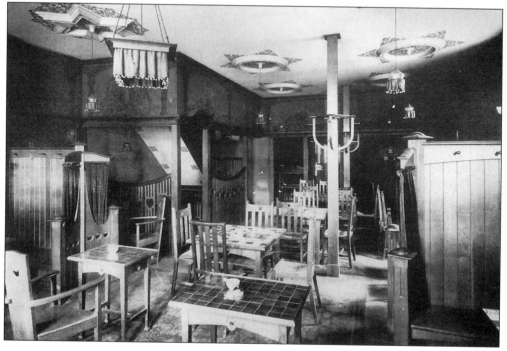

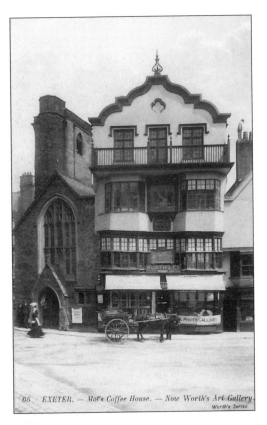

Mol's Coffee House, Cathedral Close, c.1905, by which time it had become Worth's Art Gallery. To its left is St Martin's church, which was dedicated in 1065. The graceful west window seen here was inserted by Bishop Lacey (1417-20). Below Mol's, and to its right, the Devon and Exeter Institute was once the town home of the Courtenay family. Although much of the area behind these buildings was destroyed during the 1941 raids, these architectural gems were spared.

The Royal Clarence Hotel, Cathedral Yard, seen here in around 1929, dates from 1769, when it was built by the Praed family of local bankers. St Martin's church and Mol's Coffee House, in Cathedral Close, can be seen in the background.

The West Country's answer to
Z Cars. Exeter's first police patrol car
outside the Guildhall in High Street
in 1934.

High Street, Exeter, opposite the
Queen Street entrance, in December
1958, when it was still normal to see
a policeman on duty in the city.

The Police Station and Court House in Exeter's Waterbeer Street, seen below in around 1939, were erected in 1888 at a cost of £5,000. The architect was Mr J.M. Pinn, whose original drawings are above. Waterbeare Street, which connected North Street and Goldsmith Street, running parallel with High Street, is now part of the Guildhall shopping complex. Lendon & Sons on the left were wholesale provision merchants. Exeter's CID Department was once housed at a site further left but off the picture.

Looking into High Street from Bedford Street, c.1922.

The new Head Post Office, Bedford Street, in March 1959, shortly before it opened. The post office had been in High Street (see p. 11). Even in such a comparatively short time the attractive Post Office & Savings Bank sign, along with its ER and 1959 dating, has been replaced and, many would agree, not for the better.

High Street, December 1958.

Goldsmith Street (December 1963) joined High Street just above the Guildhall, but was demolished and now forms part of the Guildhall Shopping Centre. At one stage the tiny street contained three pubs, the New Market Inn on the corner of Waterbeer Street, the Bull Inn and the Pheonix Inn.

High Street, c.1921, with St Lawrence's church on the left and the old Empire Theatre beyond it. St Lawrence's dates from 1202.

St Sidwell's church, Sidwell Street, c.1912. It was rebuilt in 1812-13 with the exception of the tower and the fourteenth-century piers of the arcade. The ten-bell peal is considered to be among the most beautiful in Devon. Destroyed during the wartime bombing, it has since been rebuilt.

STANDFIELD & WHITE

LIMITED.

Motor Body Builders and Engineers.

TELEPHONE No. 304.

Telegrams:
"Standfield White, Exeter."

Sole District Agents for

Wolseley,

Rover,

Albion,

Argyll,

and

Studebaker Cars.

Motor Bodies built to Customers' own designs.

All **Repairs** carried out by Experienced Mechanics.

Large Stock of **Tyres and Accessories.**

Landaulettes and Touring Cars for Hire.

LARGEST AND BEST EQUIPPED GARAGE
. . . IN THE WEST OF ENGLAND. . . .

8, Sidwell Street, EXETER.

Sidwell Street had a dozen floral arches like these when the Bath and West Show was held at Exeter in 1889.

Exeter's Eastgate, rebuilt by King Athelstan (924-40), was finally removed in 1784. This picture, although labelled 'Eastgate 1889' and thought to show a mock gate connected with the decorations for the Bath and West Show, held that year in Exeter (see above), might well date from Queen Victoria's Diamond Jubilee (1897). The East Gate was successfully defended against both William I and, much later, the Yorkist pretender Perkin Warbeck.

Sidwell Street following the erection of the Methodist Chapel on the left in 1905. Much of this part of the street was destroyed by the blitz, but the church and Duke of York pub survived. Sadly, some of the parts of Sidwell Street that survived were later destroyed by modern architectural vandals and new and ugly shopping blocks took their place.

W. YENDELL, = Ladies' and = Gents' Tailor,

Specialities:

Ladies' Costumes from 42/-

Gents' Breeches ,, 15/-

FOR Fit, Style, Quality, Finish, and Moderate Prices, W. YENDELL has few equals. Astonishing value is given in a two guinea Suit—the same quality is often sold at three guineas. The firm is daily adding to its connection throughout the County, customers being well satisfied and recommending others to get a first-class article at a low figure.

178, Sidwell Street, EXETER.

Branch :—4, PARIS STREET.

R.J. Hall in 1913, the Old-Established Dairy at 80 Sidwell Street, from where he 'waited on families twice daily' and was a 'Contractor to HM Government'. His adverts at the time also mention that he had 'Specially Selected Cows kept for Infants and Invalids'.

Sidwell Street, December 1958, with the Odeon Cinema dominating the skyline.

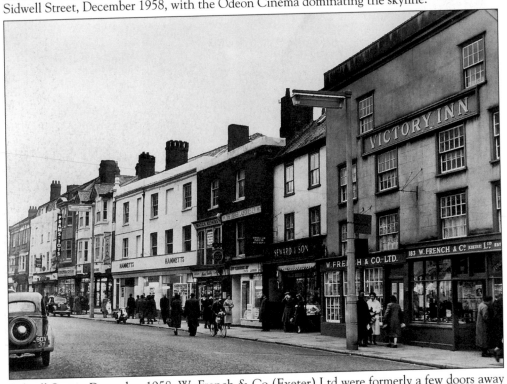

Sidwell Street, December 1958. W. French & Co (Exeter) Ltd were formerly a few doors away at nos 186-87 but then moved to the Victory Inn. The firm, along with its neighbours, Seward & Son (butchers) and Hammetts Dairies, will strike a chord in a few not-so-old memories.

Sidwell Street, December 1953. Bomb sites are now officially used as car parks. This part of the north side (on our right) of the street escaped the wartime bombing. Sadly it did not escape the post war redevelopment of the area.

The top of Sidwell Street looking into Blackboy Road, November 1957. Arthur Kempe, remembered on the drinking fountain, was a surgeon who financed a chapel in 1886 for the use of patients at the Royal Devon & Exeter Hospital at Southernhay, where he is also remembered in a stained glass west window.

Sidwell Street, 1959. Today the bus stop has been graced with a shelter and only buses and cyclists are allowed to enter this part of Sidwell Street; all other traffic heading for High Street must now turn left.

Sidwell Street, February 1958, with the York Road junction in the background and the Methodist church and Odeon Cinema beyond that. The old Timothy White's chemist shop's being currently empty is a sign of the times. Inflation has made its mark too: the pound sign (Poundstretcher) has taken over from the old threepenny and sixpenny stores (F.W. Woolworth & Co.).

Two
Queen Street
Fore Street and
Exe Bridge

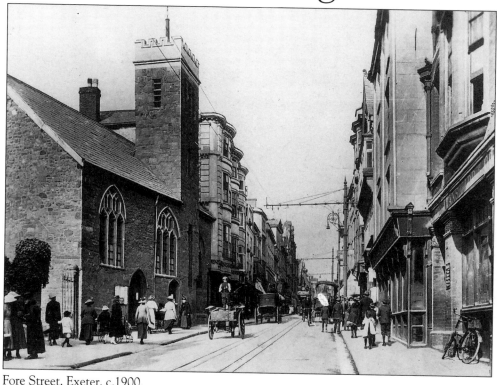

Fore Street, Exeter, c.1900.

Exe Bridge, Exeter   Valentine's Series

The first stone bridge over the Exe in Exeter was built in the thirteenth century by Walter Gervase, the mayor. It was replaced in 1788 by the bridge seen above, photographed shortly before its demolition in 1903. This was replaced in turn by a steel arch bridge designed by Sir John Wolfe Barry of Tower Bridge fame, seen below at its official opening in 1905. By the 1960s the volume of traffic and the considerable obstruction to the flow of the River Exe caused by its arches led to this bridge being replaced (see opposite).

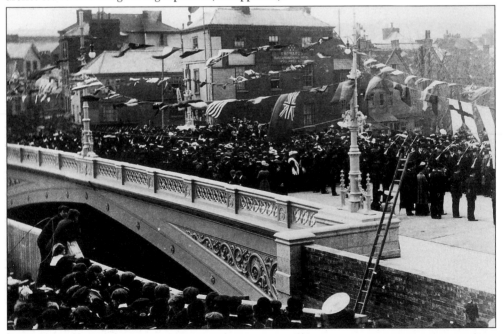

To solve the problem of increased traffic, the new Exe Bridge was in fact two bridges which fitted into the modern road network as a large roundabout straddling the river. Exe Bridge North takes the eastbound traffic, Exe Bridge South the westbound. An integral part of the design was the Flood Prevention Scheme of the Devon River Authority. The work commenced in March 1968 with Kier Limited, of Sandy, Bedfordshire, the main contractors. The piers (seen above during construction) were the most difficult part of the work because the foundation level was some sixteen feet below the water level. Exe Bridge North, with the old bridge in the background, is seen below about a month before its official opening on 30 July 1969 by the Mayor of Exeter, Alderman W.J. Hallett.

Looking across the new Exe Bridge into Exeter from St Thomas shortly after the bridge was opened in 1905.

A tram crash on Exe Bridge, 17 March 1917. No doubt the horse to the extreme left had a quiet smirk as it passed.

A traction engine accident in Fore Street, 25 April 1905. Coming just three weeks after the changeover from horse-drawn to electric trams in the city, this accident would have caused a few 'horse' laughs!

The official opening of the new bridge in 1905 found that part of Exeter *en fête*, but the 'hoi polloi' had to be kept at a respectful distance behind barriers in the background. Only the better classes have been allowed inside to be part of the real proceedings. The militia guard of honour, if the officer and his drawn sword is any indication, are supposed to be at attention, in which case they would sadden the heart of a few modern sergeant majors, what with their ragged line, their irregularly sloped weapons, and a tendency to look in all directions. The police sergeant in the middle of the picture puts them all to shame.

St Thomas, Exeter, c.1949.

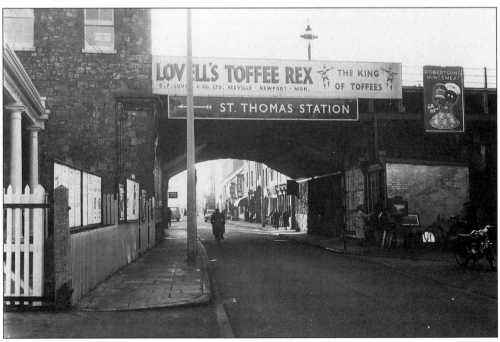

St Thomas Bridge and railway station, St Thomas, Exeter, c.1947.

Walter Otton & Sons Ltd, wholesale ironmongers of 135-138 Fore Street Hill, Exeter, in 1913.

Alphington Street, St Thomas, in around 1950 if the 1949 Hillman on the left and the A40 Countyman moving up on its inside are any guide.

Alphington Street, St Thomas, c.1959.

Looking in to Alphington Street, St Thomas, from the Exe Bridge end in about 1949. Halford's, the bicycle people, on the right, also had a branch at 31 Sidwell Street before the blitz, and are still in that street, albeit at No. 178.

T.A. Parkes, a High Class Ladies' and Gents' Tailor at 143 Fore Street, and also at the Parade, Exmouth, claimed, in 1913, that their Royal Standard Indigo Serge Suits could 'stand sea and sun'. They certainly stood comparision with today's prices, being listed at fifty shillings (£2.50), fifty-five shillings (£2.75) and sixty-three shillings (£3.15). Mr Parkes did not believe in hiding his light under a bushel. He was, according to his adverts, 'an experienced cutter ... noted for smart-fitting and well-turned suits ... Customers say they have never had better value ... Suits sold here at three guineas are frequently, elsewhere, marked up at four and five guineas ...'

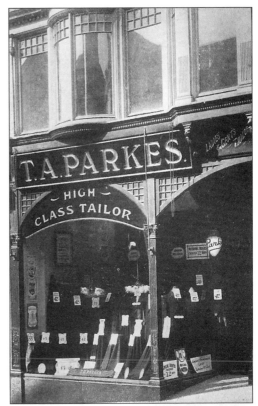

New Bridge Street looking up into Fore Street, December 1956. Grays, on the right, was a Leytonstone-based motor cycle dealers.

Fore Street, c.1955. Forte's Restaurant Snack Bar on the left had been in South Street but was destroyed during the 1941 bombing.

Fore Street, looking westwards after the air raids in 1942.

South Street, December 1959. Development has still not healed the scars of the 1942 air raids. Forte's milk shake bar, the first premises down the road on the left (see opposite), was a favourite meeting place for the younger generation.

The corner of High Street and Queen Street, in around 1932 if the Buick motor car and its Somerset (YD) registration number is any guide. It is of interest to note that the trams only turned left out of Queen Street. Wheaton's, the stationers, later moved along High Street. Masons, another well-known Exeter store, later became Huttons.

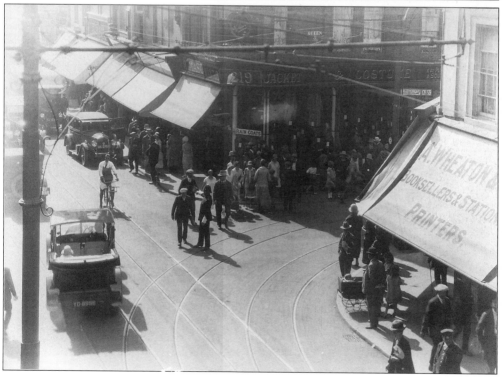

The unveiling of the Buller Statue at Bury Meadow on 6 September 1905 by the 3rd Earl Fortescue, Lord Lieutenant of Devon. A Devonian, born near Crediton in 1839, Redvers Buller had a fine military record, which included the award of the Victoria Cross during the South African War (1878-79). In common with other British generals, however, he did not appreciate that fighting white opponents (Boer War) was quite unlike operations against poorly equipped natives. The statue, in bronze, is designed by Adrian Jones. The bottom picture shows the procession approaching the statue.

The Osborne Hotel and Clock Tower, 1913. The tower was erected in 1897 to replace the Quadrangle which had stood there previously.

Mock-up of Exeter's North Gate on the Iron Bridge as part of the city's decorations for Queen Victoria's Diamond Jubilee in 1897.

Looking into Queen Street from High Street in around 1909. The picture shows the loop of the tram lines that enabled traffic to move from single-lined Queen Street into High Street, which was double-lined.

Queen Street, c.1907, with Upper Market on the rear left.

Queen Street, c.1933. Planned partly to connect the expected arrival of the railway in Exeter, Queen Street was so named in 1839, two years after the accession of Queen Victoria.

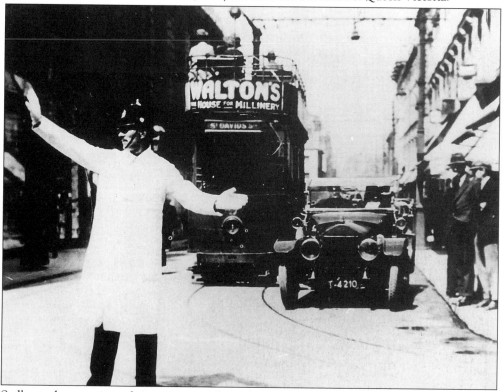

Sadly, perhaps, one no longer sees a policeman on point duty in Exeter's streets. This one, controlling the exit of traffic from Queen Street into High Street is immaculately dressed. Although the dress of the men on the right suggests a date some time around 1930, the handsome chauffeurred Rolls Royce has an early number plate and looks pre-1914. But they did make them to last after all!

The Queen Street Post Office, Exeter, September 1958.

Higher Market, Queen Street, c.1955. Exeter rid itself of its street stalls earlier than most West Country towns or cities by building a special market to house them. In Exeter's case, the street traders had cluttered both Fore Street and High Street on Tuesdays and Fridays. Higher Market was opened in 1838. Only the Doric front remains today and inside is the Guildhall Shopping Centre. Exeter's Friday market tradition is retained in the Cattle Market in Marsh Barton which was opened on 1 November 1939.

Three

Other Parts

The front of the Main Building, Royal Devon and Exeter

The Royal Devon and Exeter Hospital in Southernhay East, seen here in around 1910, moved to its present Wonford home after World War Two. It was founded in 1741, this building opening in 1743, and there have been a number of enlargements over the years.

Walter Wayland Smith, head butcher for James Blight Hannaford, whose shop at 24 North Street is seen here in around 1926.

Isca Road, St Thomas, seen here in around 1962, was built off Alphington Road in 1904 and comprised Exeter's first council houses. Forty-two 'workmen's dwellings' were built and rented at 4s 9d per week.

Freeth's Tofferies in Paris Street, seen here in the earlier 1930s, made the most of the sweets they sold. Promotional stunts included, below, this giant Easter Egg pushed home in determined manner by a small boy. Was it coincidence that amongst the traffic halted by the policeman to enable him to cross Sidwell Street was one of Freeth's Model T Ford delivery vans? Their main premises were in Sidwell Street, where they were found at numbers 14 and 56, and they also had two shops in High Street and one at 165 Fore Street.

Exeter Quay, c.1935, with the *Raycreek* moored at the quay.

Exeter Quay, from a picture by the Exeter photographer A.D. Tremlett, who, with his brother, took many pictures of Edwardian Exeter.

The Custom House Inn, Quay Lane, Exeter, c.1909.

George Sanders's fruit shop at 34 Paris Street prepares for the Christmas orders in the 1920s.

Alphington, seen here in around 1908, is to the south of the city and has a particularly fine church in St Michael's.

The aftermath of a disastrous fire at Alphington on 13 February 1909.

Countess Wear, Exeter, c.1940.

A road traffic accident at the corner of Polsloe Bridge and Pinhoe Road, c.1928.

St John's Hospital School, Exeter, c.1929. The white archway led to the High Street.

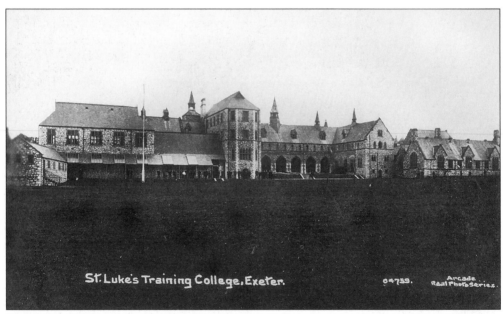

St. Luke's Training College, Exeter.   04759.   Arcade Real Photo Series.

Founded in 1838 as a Church of England Training College for Schoolmasters, St Luke's College was the oldest foundation of its kind in the United Kingdom. It suffered particularly badly during World War Two, when the main building was partially destroyed. The more recent buildings were not badly damaged, however, and, St Luke's re-opened in 1945 in both these and in new buildings which had been purchased on adjoining property. Later a new residential hostel was added and the main building was restored.

The Great
Western Hotel,
St David's
station, Exeter,
1949.

St David's Hotel,
Bonhay Road,
Exeter, seen here
before it was
demolished in
the 1920s. It
catered for the
railway trade
from nearby St
David's station.

Heavitree Bridge, c.1908.

The Livery Dole Chapel, Heavitree, c.1900.

Fore Street, Heavitree, December 1958. Heavitree ceased to be an 'independent' town in 1913 when the Heavitree UDC was incorporated in the city by the Exeter (Extension) Order.

Fore Street, Heavitree, c.1959.

Heavitree Road, looking east, before the police station was built. The lower picture shows the view in the opposite direction.

St Thomas Toc H room and the
Speedway Garage, Cowick Street,
Exeter, c.1957.

Paul Street, looking up towards Queen Street, c.1959. The Devon General Bus Station on the
left is now a car park.

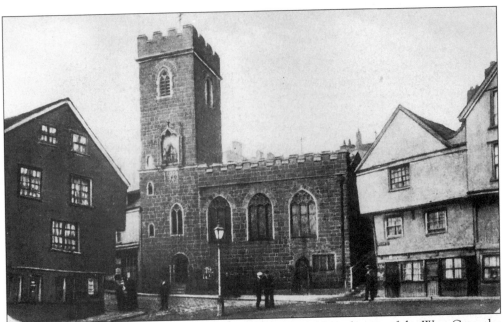

St Mary's Steps church at the foot of Stepcote Hill, c.1912. Near the site of the West Gate, the church is famous for its clock with figures that strike the hours. Said to represent Henry VIII and two javelin men, they are known locally as Matthew the Miller and his two sons.

Paris Street, c.1958. Arthur Roberts' ironmongers shop (left) and the Honiton Inn (right) were all that escaped the bombing and subsequent levelling and stand in magnificent isolation. The Honiton Inn (it stands on the road to that town) is still a popular pub. On its right is today's Civic Centre, and the car park in front is, of course, now Exeter's bus depot.

Police Headquarters, New North Road, Exeter, c.1939.

Exeter Prison, New North Road, probably in the 1920s. The prison was originally completed in 1790 but was rebuilt in 1853 on the plan of the model prison at Pentonville. The small building to the left of the main block and in front of the left-hand cell block was the execution shed. The police station (seen above) is on the extreme right.

Middlemoor Police Headquarters seen from the air shortly after its construction in 1938. Note the roundabout and the absence of traffic. The bowling green to the right of the main block is now the offices of the Chief Constable and his immediate staff. The bottom picture shows the main office block immediately after its opening.

Four

At Work ...

William Brock & Co. Ltd, Fore Street and North Street, Exeter, in around 1920, when they were probably the best-known furniture removal contractors in the city.

Hinton Lake & Son Ltd, High Street, 1949. This building dates from 1564 and was known until 1740 as the Mansion House. Shortly before this picture was taken a fourteenth-century fireplace was discovered on the first floor.

Exeter City Police Mounted Section, c.1946. Sergeant Sangster is on the left and PC Ware on the right.

Exeter City Police Ambulance Section being inspected by Commissioner Mr H.S. Bick, c.1935.

Exeter City Police Ambulance Team, c.1954. Left to right: Sgt Proctor, PC Fursman, PC Werran, PC Leyman.

Female staff with the station master at Central Station, Exeter, during Salute the Soldier Week during World War Two.

Exeter's civic leaders visiting the Infantry Record Office at Belmont Park, Exeter, at the end of World War Two to thank the staff for their work.

Exeter Home Guard at the County Ground in around 1943.

Exeter Fire Brigade, seen here with their chief William Pett, in the centre of the front row, after the Theatre Royal fire on 6 September 1906. The brigade was formed in 1888.

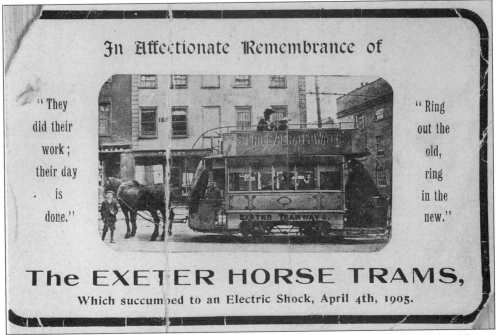

Comic cards printed to mark the passing of the Exeter horse-drawn trams on 4 April 1905.

An early Exeter electric tram in around 1910. Was it coincidence that brought a tram with a Damerel & Son advert to that firm's 161 Sidwell Street premises?

Queueing in Exeter during World War One.

Women working on the harvest at Exeter during World War One.

Weapons being cleaned at the Exeter Territorial Armoury in Longbrook Street in around 1910.

Frank Moore, his wife Lilian and son Frank (Jun.) with some of the nursing staff at the Redhills Workhouse in 1916 when it was in use as a military hospital.

Chief Inspector John Skinner wearing an original pattern helmet in around 1888. Note the vent at the top of the helmet.

Exeter City Police marching along High Street to St Mary Arches church in 1953. The three officers at the front are, from left to right: Inspector Moore, Detective Inspector Pessell, Inspector Lightfoot.

An Exeter fireman photographed at the turn of the century by the well-known Exeter photographer H. Faulkner White at his studio at 173 Sidwell Street.

Firemen tackle a blaze at Central Station, Queen Street, (then on the L&SWR line) during the 1930s. During the operation one of the firemen was injured after falling from the roof of the main building.

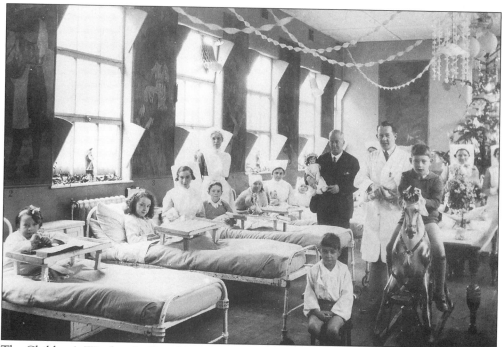

The Children's Ward at the Royal Devon and Exeter Hospital in 1936.

The Radiography Room at the Royal Devon and Exeter Hospital in around 1910. No doubt considered the latest in its field at the time, it looks primitive by today's standards.

One of the larger police boxes once found in Exeter. This one was beside the River Exe near Exe Bridge.

A handsome row of police cars (and men) at the old Police Station in Waterbeer Street in the 1950s.

Some police boxes were much smaller, so much so that Dr Who would have been hard pushed to turn one into a Tardis! The one seen here stood at the junction of Paris Street and Heavitree Road where PC Nordquist poses for a publicity photograph.

Police Constables Cole and Webber are the members of this Exeter City Police patrol car escorting an abnormal load on the Exeter bypass in February 1949.

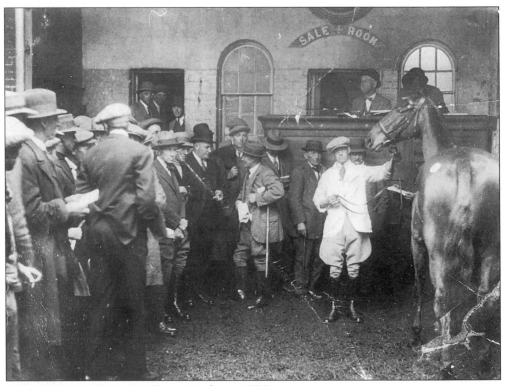

Hussey's Auction Rooms at Exeter Market, c.1926.

Exeter Cattle Market, 1898.

A.E. 'Albert' Appleby outside his fish shop at 10 Queen Street, c.1919. The shop stood to the south side of the entrance to Higher Market. The little boy in the foreground was drowned some four or five years later while swimming at Dawlish Warren.

Peter Slader & Son Ltd, Southernhay East, Exeter, were prominent fruit merchants in the city. One of their earlier ventures into motorized deliveries was this American Real Speedwaggon, seen here in the mid-1930s.

TEETH! TEETH!! TEETH!!!

PAINLESS DENTISTRY.

CONSULTATIONS FREE.

Teeth Extracted, Painless, from **1/-**   Artificial Teeth from **5/-** per Tooth.
Teeth Stopped from **2/6** each.   Teeth Scaled from **1/-** each.

SETS SCALED COMPLETE FROM £1 1s.
ARTIFICIAL SETS OF TEETH (PRIZE MEDAL) FROM £3 10s.

MR. SANDERS

HAVING made extensive alterations in his Mechanical Rooms, and having added all the latest improvements in Modern Dentistry—the same as being shown at the **AMERICAN EXHIBITION, LONDON**—is now able, with his efficient staff of Assistants, to manufacture Sets of Artificial Teeth complete in twenty-four hours. All repairs to artificial work can be done while the patient is waiting.

MR. SANDERS will personally attend all patients between the hours of 9.30 a.m. and 7 p.m. Engagements can be made for a later hour by letter or telegram.

Daily Attendance from 9 a.m to 9 p.m.

C. H. SANDERS, R.D.S.,

DENTAL-SURGEON,

88, QUEEN STREET, EXETER.

(OPPOSITE THE MARKET.)

No Branch Establishment in the City.   VACANCY FOR A PUPIL.

Mr Sanders was one of many Exeter trade and professional persons who advertised in the 1887 programme for a Fancy Fair held in aid of the fund for the erection of a Drill Hall for the 1st Volunteer Battalion Devonshire Regiment, formed as the First Rifle Volunteers in 1852. One doubts whether his promise of 'painless dentistry' would get past today's more rigorous advertising standards.

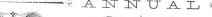
Henry S. Eland, High Street, Exeter, announcing his 'examples of the Christmas Cards of every maker ... including the Finest Specimens of Chromo-lithography ...' was one of the city's leading stationers. The family name is retained in today's Exeter business world by his grandson Bob, who runs a similar business in Bedford Street.

Timber ships discharging their cargoes at Exeter Dock in November 1960 for Rawle, Gammon & Baker Ltd. Below, the tanker *Ben Johnson* passes through the locks on Exeter Canal in 1955. This was the first lock canal built in England. Isabella, Countess of Devon, fell out with the city fathers over the sale of fish and built a weir across the river below the city (hence Countess Wear). This forced ships to unload at Topsham which was much to that town's, and of course the Countess's, benefit. Exeter's city fathers tried to get round it by building the canal between 1564-67.

Haymes, part of Exeter's business world since 1824, was a well-established and respected Court and Military Bootmakers when this picture of their premises at 16 Cathedral Yard was taken in 1912.

They may be members of Exeter City Police, but that does not stop Inspector 'Tiny' Turner and PC T. Hancock from getting out into the countryside during an outbreak of foot-and-mouth disease. The date? Well the 1932 Austin Six looks pretty new.

Anyone who has known the dubious pleasure of fatigues, during either wartime or post-war National Service in the forces, will sympathise with this body of men. They are a fatigue party formed from recruits of the Exeter City Police at Police HQ, New North Road, in 1930.

Devon's Chief Constable, Major L.H. Morris (right), with members of the Women's Auxiliary Police Corps at Middlemoor during World War Two.

George VI receives the sword of state from the Mayor of Exeter, Alderman J.G.R. Orchard, on the arrival of the royal party at St David's station in 1950. The sword was presented to the city by Henry VII in 1497, when he arrived in person to thank Exeter for resisting the seige of Perkin Warbeck, a Yorkist pretender who claimed to be Richard IV. It is said that Henry occupied the treasurer's house from where he ordered sixteen trees in the Close to be removed so that he might see from the window the rebels who were brought before him to plead successfully for mercy and pardon.

The funeral procession of Inspector Rounsley of Exeter City Police passes under Polsloe Bridge, Exeter, in 1939.

Mrs J. Morrish, wife of the Chief Constable of Devon, Major L.H. Morrish, cuts the first sod at the site of the new police headquarters at Middlemoor in 1938. (See p. 70.)

The Windsor Hotel, Exeter, c.1941.

Animal exhibits being delivered to the Royal Albert Memorial Museum in Bedford Street, c.1912. The museum, built at a cost of around £20,000, was founded in 1869 as a memorial to the Prince Consort. It has been substantially added to since.

The Bowring Ward (Children), Royal Devon and Exeter Hospital, c.1910. This ward was provided and paid for by Mrs J.C. Bowring for young children.

The evicted papermills strikers' camp at Stoke Canon in 1915. The workers, members of the National Union of Printing & Paper Workers, had gone on strike for better wages and union recognition. Their employer, C. Tremlett, refused their demands and evicted fourteen families from their cottages. The unions provided the tents and raised money by selling this postcard.

Exeter Assize Sunday, c.1951.

General Sir Ian Hamilton, President of the (Royal) British Legion, second left, about to leave from Exeter airport after an official visit to Devon in 1938. On the right is the airport manager Flt Lt R.L. Bateman.

Bomb damage in Okehampton Street, 1942.

Prospect Park after the 1942 raids. The house on the right (rear) belonged to Mr Ernest Oswald Harding, the architect.

The Bath & West Show at Exeter, 1909.

Exeter Market, 1936.

Her Majesty Queen Elizabeth II received the red carpet treatment when she arrived at Exeter University on 8 June 1956 to unveil the foundation stone of the new arts building. She is accompanied by the Chancellor of the University, Mary, Duchess of Devonshire.

The port of Exeter shortly after the turn of the century.

Queen Street on a wet day in 1955. Nothing much changes in the upper storeys, seen here, but there has been an almost complete change in the names above the shop windows.

St James' Infants School, c.1903. The teacher on the left is a Miss Greenslade.

A fire in Queen Street in 1910 attracts a large crowd.

J. & G. ROSS

Clerical Tailors and Outfitters

A familar feature in Exeter's pre-war High Street, J. & G. Ross would have plenty of customers today if they were still offering their 'Roscut' pure wool and waterproof coats for ladies and gentlemen at fifty-five shillings.

Hoopern Street School, Exeter, c.1924. Among the children seen here are Kathleen Pegler (now Stirzaker), Jack Pearce, next to her, and next again is Evelyn Pearce (no relation). The mistress is Miss Hitchcock. Others include Nancy Slade and Freda Carter.

Bradley Rowe School, Exeter, 1936. Back row, left to right: -?-, ? Young, Bert Sharland, Violet Lyne. Third row: Jean Snapso, Doris Kemp, -?-, ? Bates. Second row: Donald Palmer, Betty Parris, ? Russell, -?-. Front: Archie Hitchcock, -?-, ? Baker, Lil Stone.

Five

... at Play

Mount Radford School outing, July 1908.

Exeter City Football Club, 1913-14. Back row, left to right: S. Greenway (trainer), A. Norman Kendall, A. Chadwick (manager), J.I. Pengelly, W. Norman, G.A. Middleweek, S.H. Thomas (secretary). Third row: E. Lewis, R. Loram, R. Gerrish, W. Kirby, R. Pym, S. Strettle, A. Evans, F. Hunt, J. Manaton, -?- (groundsman). Second row: F. Whittaker, J. Fort, J. Rigby, Mr M.J. McGahay (chairman), W. Smith, F. Marshall, H. McCann, J.C. Lee. Front: H. Holt, C. Pratt, F. Lovett, J. Lagan, H. Orr, J. Goddard.

Vedrine's arrival at Exeter during the *Daily Mail* Air Contest around 1910.

Members of Exeter Camera Club outside the Trout Inn, Bickleigh, April 1891.

The 1st Exeter Boys' Brigade, c.1897.

Heavitree Church Sunday School Outing, 25 June 1924.

An outing for an unknown destination leaves from outside the County Steam Laundry at 38 Longbrook Street, Exwick.

An unspecified outing to an unknown destination, c.1928. In front is Mrs C.E. Murch, the wife of the sub-Postmaster at Clifton Road Post Office; third left is Mrs Russell, whose husband was a well-known police officer in Exeter.

Trippers in around 1905 about to start their trip down the Exeter Canal to Turf, a popular spot at the confluence of the canal and the River Exe. It was particularly noted for the excellence of whitebait teas on offer there.

Exeter Cycling Club, 1909, at the County Ground. Back row, left to right: A.E.R. Brett, H. Bright, T.J. Mooney, C. Samuels, G.E. Young, A. Agnew, T.W. Webber, F. Crook, P. Hexter, T.H. Hayes, W.E. Piper, F. Balsom. Third row: T. Neal, M. Gilpin, J. Wills, G.H. Vooght, T. Coles, T. Howard, G.H. Conibear, F. Leyman, W.G. Stevenson, C.C. Harvey, R. Otton, W.J.S. Lisle, A.J. Andrews, S.B. Barrington, J. Flood. Second row: E. Stephens, N.T. Dray, F. Chick, J.C. Cole, W.H. Rudd, S.C. Cole, F.W. Wood, J.H. Brown, Dr Brash, H. Oxenham, H.T. Hems, A.J. Connett, F.K. Sharland, F.G. Towill, F.R. Bowden. Front: F.E. Bowden, W. Down, H.P. Overmass, W.A. Bayley, F.S. Shobbrook, W.G. Hodge, J. Peters, W.G. Kallaway, W.H. Ayear, J.H. Stile, A.B. Norman, F. Sandy.

Old Timers' Association of Exeter Cycling Club, 26 May 1929. Standing, left to right: J.H. Bartlett, A.J. Connett, A. Agnew. Middle: H.T. Hems, E. Stevens, A.J. Andrew, A.N. Pitts, G. Coldridge, P. Hexter, F.R. Bowden, F.E. Bowden. Front: T. Lambooy, F.K. Sharland, J.H. Brown, F. Chick, E. Chick, F.G. Towill, W.A. Bayley, W.H. Rudd, F.W. Wood. Most of the above had joined the club before 1900; Mr E. Chick in the front row had been a member since 1885.

The Exeter Cycling Club, seen here in around 1879, was formed in 1873. According to the secretary, Mr W.H. Casley, in his annual report in 1885, it had thirty-nine members and was one of the oldest clubs in the country. It could claim descent from the Exeter Bicycle Club which held road events, club runs and racing. Fifty-seven members served in World War One but, following a very successful Golden Jubilee year in 1923, the club disbanded in the mid-1920s. Its successor was today's Exeter Wheelers Cycling Club which was formed in 1924. For many years the old cycling club met at its own clubhouse (below) in Sidwell Street which was destroyed during the 1942 air raids and is now the site of Tesco.

Exeter Cycling Club's tableau which won third prize in the 1912 Exeter Pageant.

Exeter Wheelers Cycling Club's first official photograph on 14 September 1924, soon after its formation. Members include Cyril Lang, Arthur Elston, Hilda Langdon, Winifred Elston, Fred Ebdon, John Steer, Harold Steer, Bill Steer, William Elston, Harry Lang, Alice Elston, Edgar Spray. This picture was taken at Streatham Hill in New North Road, where the club held their 10-mile races.

Exeter Cycling Club, c.1900.

Exeter Wheelers Cycling Club's first Sports Meeting at St James's Park, Exeter, on 21 May 1934. They held them there in 1934, 1935 and 1936 but the cycling events were impractical on a football ground and the club moved to the County Ground, where a special track had been made for cycling. Left to right: Frank Gibbons, Tommy Grigg, -?-, Arthur Elston (secretary), -?-, Fred Wood (President), Charles Ross, -?-, William Elston, -?-, -?-, George Rice (Exeter City FC Supporters Club).

Quite a few empty seats at Exeter City's St James's Park ground, even for the visit of Devon rivals Plymouth Argyle for an old Southern League game in 1910-11.

There was a crowd of 12,000 to watch the Devon-Durham Rugby County Championship final at Exeter RFC's County Ground in April 1907. The teams drew 0-0 and the title was shared.

An Exeter Liberal Party outing to Minehead leaves from the Cathedral Yard on 3 July 1922.

Exeter City Police members set off on their annual outing to Weymouth on 19 July 1926. The journey, if the 12 m.p.h. limit in force at the time was obeyed, would have taken over four hours. And with a charabanc full of coppers, the driver would have had to watch his speed.

The directors and staff at Exeter Hippodrome, c.1925.

C Division rifle team, Exeter Police Force, c.1914. Just as King George V felt compelled to change his Germanic family name of Saxe-Coburg to the very English Windsor for patriotic reasons during the wave of somewhat paranoid 'Hun Hating' that swept the country during World War One, Superintendent De Schmid (centre front) changed his as well, but to what is now unknown.

The Pups 4th annual outing ready to leave from the Trust House, Exeter (now the Great Western Hotel) on 24 June 1923.

Workers at the old Exeter Gas, Light and Coke Company in 1923, when their works were at the City Basin. Their offices were in Southernhay East.

Dellers waitresses during World War Two.

Church Parade of the Rose of Devon Lodge (RAOB) in Sidwell Street in 1957. Post-war reconstruction of bomb sites can be seen going on in the background. Third from left in the front is Provincial Grand Primo Arthur Wilson.

Happy smiling faces on the ladies from the Wonford Inn in Wonford Street who are preparing to leave for an outing in 1949. Herbert Pritchard was the landlord at the time.

Elizabeth II's coronation in June 1953 was marked in Exeter by, among other things, a service in the Cathedral. The procession seen here leaving by the west door is headed by Walter Daw, the Sheriff, Alderman Alfred Bovey, the Mayor, and C.J. Newman, the Town Clerk. The ornate west window is generally considered to be the most beautiful window in the Decorated style in England. It now has glass which was put in in 1904 in memory of Frederick Temple, Bishop of Exeter and later Archbishop of Canterbury.

Wonford Inn darts team, cup winners and league runners-up, 1948-49.

The GWR football club team, c.1954. Between 1947 and 1949 GWR won the Football Express Cup three times in succession. The team seen here is, back row, left to right: Arthur Ford, Bert Chave (linesman), Dusty Miller, Ken Ford, Bob Christie, Ian Pollard, Reg Wotton (trainer), Gil Driver. Front: Tom Connett, Bill Diamond, Des Gooding, Jim Hull, Keith Miller.

Princess Elizabeth with the Mayor of Exeter, Mr William Wills, inspecting St John Ambulance Brigade nursing cadets at Topsham Barracks in November 1946.

Ladysmith School football team, 1929-30. Back row, left to right: Mr Yeoman, Ted Hodgeson, Jim Spike, Bert Stoneman, Jim Quance, Jim Burrows, Reg Pyne. Middle: Charlie Martin, Wilf Combes, Charlie Setter, Bob Chandler, Wally Petherick, Fred Chudley. Front: Les Gale, Lloyd Matthews.

VJ Day Party at Whipton Institute, 1945.

St Matthew's Air Scouts on Church Parade in 1943 pass the Axminster Inn in Paris Street. Sadly, neither the inn nor its City Ales are with us today.

City Brewery staff party at Dellers Cafe in around 1922.

Bob Shepherd receives his fireman's long-service award from the Mayor of Exeter, Rowland Glave Saunders, during World War Two.

Raddan's Printing Works at 21-22 Combe Street throw a party to celebrate George VI's coronation in May 1937.

Staff of Gabriel, Wade & English's Timber Yard in Exeter leave for an outing in 1947. The firm, situated at Shilhay in Commercial Road, were well-known timber importers and supplied every kind of timber to the building trade.

George VI
Coronation Street
Party at Pound Street,
Exeter, in 1937.

WVS Party in the Old
Civic Hall, Queen
Street, January 1943.

Nurses carolling around the wards at the Royal Devon and Exeter Hospital, c.1952.

Smiling faces following the issue of a special food ration in Exeter during World War One.

Beacon Avenue Railway Club Outing, c.1952.

The first annual staff outing for the Palladium Cinema, Exeter, on 27 July 1930. The cinema, listed as the Palladium Cinematograph Theatre in city directories, was at 93-94 Paris Street.

Exeter's VJ Parade in 1945.

Alphington ringers, 1948.

The HEAVITREE BREWERY Ltd.
EXETER.

GOLD MEDAL

OATMEAL STOUT

18, 9, and 5 Gallon
Casks, 21/-, 10/6,
and 5/10.

In Bottles,
2/6 dozen pints,
1/6 dozen half-pints.

Reduced facsimile of
Grand Prix and Gold Medal
awarded The Heavitree
Brewery at Paris for their
Celebrated Oatmeal Stout.

Acknowledgements

We are especially grateful to Chris Wright, librarian at the *Express & Echo*, and to the paper's editor, Rachael Campey, for permission to research and make use of its extensive collection of old pictures of Exeter.

Also to the Chief Constable, Mr John Evans, for permission to use items from the Force (Devon & Cornwall Constabulary) Museum and to the curator Brian Estill for his help and for an interesting and personal tour of the many exhibits in the museum.

Also to Jim Cook for taking the time to tell us about the Exeter of his boyhood days.

Others who allowed us to use their pictures were Jean Luxton and Exeter Wheelers, Alf and Marian Roberts, Nan Steel, Kathleen Stirzaker, Barbara Sutton and Roger Taylor and the Exeter Camera Club. Our thanks to them all.

We would like to thank the staff of Chalford Publishing, and especially Simon Thraves, for putting up with us.